REDESIGNING HIGHER TECHNICAL EDUCATION TO MEET NATIONAL ASPIRATIONS

REDESIGNING HIGHER TECHNICAL EDUCATION TO MEET NATIONAL ASPIRATIONS

Prof Chandan Tilak Bhunia

ISBN: 978-93-5128-136-8

Price : ₹ 360

First Published, 2016

Published by

Kalpaz Publications
C-30, Satyawati Nagar,
Delhi – 110052
E-mail: kalpaz@hotmail.com
Ph.: 9212142040

Printed at: G. Print Process, Delhi

Cataloging in Publication Data—DK

Courtesy: D.K. Agencies (P) Ltd. <docinfo@dkagencies.com>

Bhunia, C. T., 1958- **author.**

Redesigning higher technical education to meet national aspirations / Prof Chandan Tilak Bhunia.

pages cm

Includes bibliographical references.

ISBN 9789351281368

1. Education, Higher—India. 2. Technical education—India. 3. North Eastern Regional Institute of Science and Technology. I. Title.

LA1153.B48 2015 DDC 378.54 23

Dedicated to:

Shyamsundarpur R. K Vidyapith; Jalchak N.N Vidyalaya; R. K. M Vivekananda Centenary College; University of Calcatta and Jadavpur University.

Contents

Preface

"If you look at history, innovation does not come just from giving people incentives; it comes from creating environments where their ideas can connect"—

—Steveen Johnson

In order to achieve competitive advantages in the current scenario of liberalization, privatization and globalization; qualitative and innovative Higher Technical Education is prime for any developing country. It is firmly believed that reshaping and redesigning of Technical Higher Education in India is of paramount importance for making "New India". In this context, this book proposes a few innovative solutions for making Technical Higher Education purposeful, meaningful and deliverable for the country. Main emphasis is given on—"Redesigning Syllabus"; "Reformatting Examination System"; "Innovations in Faculty Recruitment Scheme" and "Innovation in changing mindset of the students".

My thoughts portrayed in this book got published as several articles in University News. This book compiles the published and some unpublished articles in the form of book. All the ideas, thoughts and comments given in the book are in my own personal capacity and not in official capacity in any way.

Date: 25.07.2015 ***Prof. C.T. Bhunia***

Introduction

"Education is first, economy next", and "economy is most important for a country not missile". These are absolute simple laws of development for any country. The Country needs to make a plan for inclusive education, for inclusive growth and for inclusive economy. Further, any Inclusive Education Policy should be and would be importantly innovative and essentially country-specific rather than a copied version of that of any other country or a mixture of copies of someother countries. In the field of education, there are several components such as Elementary Education, School Education, College Education and University Education. Again, education is classified as humanities, science, commerce, technical etc. In the history of development, it is clearly, fairly and squarely revealed that the appropriate application of Science and Technology is at the core. Central Social Research has been searching for a solution for removing the gap between the "haves" and "havenots". Scientific and Technological solutions in respect of removing socialgaps are major instruments.

Therefore, Science and Technological Education of any country should be given priority to reduce the gap between peoples' expectations and priorities of the Government. Over decades, the Technical Education system imparted in India is seen to yield not substantial deliverable outputs to meet the aspirations of the country and its citizens. Therefore, there emerges out an urgency to look into the reasons for failures of our existing Technical Education system and thereby to re-devise the system to be a deliverable system measured by return on investment. Re-shaped and re-designed Technical Education system should be deliverable and meaningful to the country.

The participation of India in the global process of liberalisation, privatisation and globalisation has created enormous opportunities subject to careful exercise for application. World, over the history, has witnessed two clear divisions. Capital intensive group and Labour intensive group; no one being the replacement of the other, but essentially supplement to each other. It is an absolute self-murder and political blunder to copy and apply the policies of one group to another group and vice-versa. Fact is that for the labour-intensive country like India, the success plan will definitely and decisively be:

- "Grow More Food" for economy.
- "Enhance Human Resources" for competitive advantage particularly in the age of LPG.

By no stretch of imagination, it can be said that India has ever exercised LPG judiciously and appropriately to cater to the needs for success in country-specific modes and means.

At the same time, priority assigned to generate and enhance human resources and research in science and technology particularly by public investment is found to be insignificant compared to other investments. Therefore, and thereby, there is an immediate need to look for a massive quick and smart approach for:

(a) Reshaping and redesigning Technical Education in India; and

(b) Devising some novel scheme for more investment in Technical Education.

With Liberalisation, Privatisation and Globalisation in midst of revolution of Information Technology (IT), the world has witnessed a radical changed scenario. Before IT Revolution, the countries in the world used to be classified in two parameters: GDP (Gross Domestic Product) / GNP(Gross National Product) on economy and HDI (Human Development Index) on human resources. IT (Information Technology) has added a new parameter of classification of countries by "information rich" and "information poor", the common name of division being known as digital divide. Fact is that IT has created enormous opportunities not without creating painful gap between the countries. The challenges of reducing the gaps created by IT requires enhancement, in both subjective and objective manners and intelligent capability of a country.

Therefore, generation of improved as well innovative Science and Technology Education is essentially most important for the developing countries; attempts so far exercised by copying the system and structure of the developed countries have proven to yield no result so far and if continued, will be suicidal in nature. This calls for reshaping Technical Education in India in totality for achieving the expected result.

Currently in the process of imparting technical education in India, there are basically two layers of system: Prestigious Institutes of National Importance (IITs/NITs/IISERs) and AICTE-approved institutes (including Central/State Govt./Private Universities and Colleges). Liberalisation, Globalisation and Privatisation in which India entered since 1992, have opened up great challenges, viabilities and potentialities subject to adoption and changes. Generation of a deliverable brilliant pool of national human resources is decisively a sound strategy for any developing country for competitive advantage in the current globalised economy. Economy and Education are most important for any country, and these are dependent on each other; but not replacement. Today like never before, national development is closely related to the application of Science and Technology in the developmental process.

The wisdom of being developed is, therefore, how exceptionally fine are the national intelligent resources and how closely generation system of human resources fit the national requirement. India despite claiming to be the third largest technical manpower in the world, has not yielded the expected results. This calls for reviewing of current technical education system of India towards devising mechanism for result-oriented transformation and to lay emphasis on "Return on Investment" made by the country.

The current technical education in India is objectively placed, of course not limited to, by just producing: (i) in general, "academic engineers" rather than "technical engineers" (ii) in generating engineers who in general run after jobs rather than building minds to create at least certain jobs (iii) in providing "memorised" education rather than "igniting thought process" in-built in a student and (iv) in imparting education without values and ethics and without a holistic approach. What is strongly, quickly and massively needed is surely a changed, innovative and country specific model. Innovations are the need of the hour in regard to framing a syllabus to meet the aspirations of applying products of the system to build a developed India.

Out of many inputs that require innovations, first and foremost is the need of framing unique syllabi for promising Technical Education. The emphasise requires to be made on the value of "practice is the first theory" in teaching and "credit and time structure is for content and content is not for structure, i.e., not fixing content of any course in a time-bound structure".

In designing the contents of any subject paper, "then should be higher emphasis given to thinking and imagination process over memorising process" in teaching mechanism creating a "do while learning" environment, "entrepreneurship teaching" as essentiality, "human values, ethics, NCC and NSS" for holistic man-making, and finally, changing the evaluation process from current practice on "how much you do not know" to "how much you know." The introduction of on-line examination both for objective and subjective evaluation and open book examination will be very much rational in this context.

In this context, some concrete innovations suggested below may be incorporated:

(i) Two models of teaching called as J.C. Bose Model and as S.N. Bose Model may be introduced. In each semester one-half of the subject papers of each discipline may be taught in the J.C. Bose Model with teaching philosophy of practices is the first theory, meaning that the papers should be taught in practical classes mostly. Under S.N. Bose model the courses may be taught in philosophy of "theory is the first practice" whereupon one-half of subject papers may be taught in a mix of theory and practical classes as in conventional teaching.

(ii) One of the subject papers in each semester in all departments may be taught as industrial course whereupon 50 per cent of the course content may be taught by an industrial expert. These attempts may make students more practical oriented rather than academic minded.

(iii) For all disciplines, a subject paper on entrepreneurship practice should be mandatory to promote entrepreneurship enthusiasm among the students.

(iv) Besides one mandatory course on "Research Paper Communication/Innovation Practice" may be introduced in all under graduate programmes to enhance the inherent thinking power of the students.

(v) Two compulsory papers namely; "NCC and NSS" and "values and ethics" should be introduced in all under graduate programmes to make the students physically fit and mentally sound.

(vi) Several add-on courses should be offered to the students during vacation as optional to qualifying for enhancing the employability of students.

(vii) Many audit papers on communication skill may be offered by visiting professors on Japanese, French etc.

(viii) The examination process should be mentioned in the syllabus. The examination system should be conventional type, online examination and open book. Question papers should be prepared such that students are evaluated to examine how much they know rather than how much they do not know. This is simply possible by setting paper of more (say 150) than maximum marks (say 100) and asking students to answer whatever they can and keeping the maximum score limited to whatever they score or maximum mark (100) whichever is lower.

1

Creation of Opportunities for Higher Education in Equitable Manner

Creation of opportunities for higher education is brilliant, whereas creation in equitable manner in respect of intake on pro-rata basis with population is undoubtedly a strength. As of now, all States in the country are having each a prestigious Institute of National Importance, viz. National Institute of Technology at the initiative of the Central Government. Nothing can be more exceptionally rewarding than such creation for the noble cause of intelligent human resources in the country. The stated approach is emphatically fair for equal growth and availability of higher education spread over entire geographical location of the country and providing a guarantee to each state having an institute like National Institute of Technology.

However, the exceptionally credible exercise undertaken by the Central Government would be more applauding and appealing, had it also looked into the issue of offering equal opportunities in an equitable manner with respect to population of states. The discrepancy is evident in the (Table – I) portraying the total seats (which is a fundamental measure of availability) available in all states to the aspiring youths.

In the (Table – I), 50 per cent of intake reserved (or at least may be filled up by the candidates of the state) is taken as the parameter of sure availability to reasonably assumed 0.10 per cent of state population (as candidates) seeking for admission. Therefore, the probability of getting chance is calculated and shown in the last column of the Table. It is found that states which are above the country average are mainly small states like Arunachal Pradesh, Nagaland, Tripura etc., and those below are mainly bigger states like Uttar Pradesh, Bihar, West Bengal etc. In general, big States are worst sufferers.

Several proposals may be thought of in resolving the stated imbalance in providing opportunities of higher education to the youths of the country in an equitable manner.

Firstly, for bigger states, the seat reservation may be 75 per cent of the intake; whereas smaller states may continue with 50 per cent. There is of course an inherent disadvantage in the proposal. The proposal may regionalise the national character which is of vital importance in any NIT.

Secondly, the Government may think of establishing more than one NIT in big states. The proposal requires the bigger investment which is a matter of concern. This seems to be the best option.

Thirdly, removing state based Reservation Policy in all NITs and giving equal opportunities to all youths in an environment of "Seats for the Best".

To my personal thinking, the third proposal appears to be difficult for the states to accept logically and at the same time, to provide some initial advantage to the North-Eastern Region the present Reservation Policy may continue in the NITs of North-Eastern Region for a seed period of about five years. After all, all of us want NITs to be "Anything but ordinary". That is required for the sake of making India extraordinary in human resources.

Table 1

NITs 50% Intake State-wise Report

NITs 50% of Intake / 0.10% of Population Report				
Sl. No	**State NIT**	**50% Intake in Engineering**	**0.10% of State Population**	**Ratio (50% of Intake: 0.10% of population)**
1	NIT - Agartala	433	3671	0.11795
2	MN NIT - Allahabad	407	199581	0.00204
3	NIT - Arunachal Pradesh	75	1382	0.05427
4	MANIT - Bhopal	468	72597	0.00645
5	NIT - Calicut	485	33387	0.01453
6	NIT - Delhi	90	16753	0.00537
7	NIT - Durgapur	423	91347	0.00463
8	NIT - Goa	45	1457	0.03089
9	NIT - Hamirpur	284	6856	0.04142
10	MNIT - Jaipur	355	68621	0.00517
11	Dr BRANIT - Jalandhar	438	27704	0.01581
12	NIT - Jamshedpur	300	32966	0.00910
13	NIT - Kurukshetra	416	25353	0.01641
14	NIT - Manipur	75	2721	0.02756
15	NIT - Meghalaya	75	2964	0.02530
16	NIT - Mizoram	60	1091	0.05500
17	NIT - Nagaland	45	1980	0.02273
18	VNIT - Nagpur	373	112372	0.00332
19	NIT - Patna	308	103804	0.00297
20	NIT - Puducherry	45	1244	0.03617
21	NIT - Raipur	477	25540	0.01868
22	NIT - Rourkela	450	41947	0.01073
23	NIT - Sikkim	60	607	0.09885
24	NIT - Silchar	302	31169	0.00969
25	NIT - Srinagar	316	12548	0.02518
26	SUNIT - Surat	363	60383	0.00601
27	NIT - Surathkal	370	61130	0.00605
28	NIT - Tiruchirappalli	407	72138	0.00564
29	NIT - Uttarakhand	150	10116	0.01483
30	NIT - Warangal	370	84655	0.00437
		8465	1208084	
	National Intake:	0.00701		
(Total 50% Intake / 0.10% of Total State Population				

2

Ways to Preserve the Brilliant Innovations In-built in NERIST System

The Technical Education in the country is conducted by four tiers of institutes namely: Indian Institutes of Technology (IITs) and National Institutes of Technology (NITs) (Institutes of National Importance); Central Universities; Deemed and State Universities and private colleges and universities, 18 IITs, 30 NITs and about 44 Central Universities are imparting Technical Education in conventional mode having no innovations in structures since the inception of system of Technical Education in the country. Only structural innovations in imparting Technical Education started with the establishment of North Eastern Regional Institute of Science and Technology (NERIST) in 1986 in Arunachal Pradesh.

The Project of NERIST is not only innovative in character but also a most fitting system of education to a country like India. The NERIST model is cost-effective and efficient model for India. The concept of NERIST is the brain child of Prof Amitabh Bhattacherjee, Eminent Scientist and a Former Director, IIT, Kanpur. The system was devised and proposed out of decisive findings that the existing conventional system of Technical Education is tuned to produce "Academic Engineers" rather than

"Practical Engineers." It is also understood that India not being a very rich country needs to design a cost-effective system of Technical Education. Affordability of high cost of higher education is always a stumbling block for a country like ours. In the light of above, two significant and important findings, NERIST is supposed to be an extraordinarily unique, brilliantly innovative and exceptionally aspiring project conceived and established for the first time in India. NERIST is offering a modular structure of education: "Base", "Diploma" and "Degree" each of two years duration. It is inherently a three-in-one institute (ITI + Polytechnic + College/University).

Running three levels of Technical Education in one institute is conclusively a cost effective system of education. Producing BTech Engineers (those who want knowledge of why) after Diploma and Base (providing knowledge of how) surely and certainly make the BTech Engineers of NERIST more practical than Engineers of the other institutes. Besides, an exposure of continuous and long six years in the Technical Education System in NERIST with house full of laboratories adds required values to practical knowledge so earned.

Basic philosophy and the uniqueness of NERIST must be preserved at any cost for sheer benefits of the country. Problems arising out if any need to be solved by scientific and logical application of mind. The country in general and Technical Education in particular, will fail miserably to perform the responsibility bestowed upon it if it failed in sustaining art, innovations and uniqueness so framed no in the NERIST projects. With modular system of Technical Education, the three modules are operative and meaningful only with vertical mobility and horizontal terminality. Any attempt not to implement horizontal terminality thereby and making the system as only of six years BTech, will be suicidal in nature being not-seen-before already having a fine educational structure in-built in NERIST apart from being first ever established concept in the whole of India.

It is understood that three-module structure is at stake because of obvious aspirations and expectations of the students admitted in Base Module. All students admitted in Base Module like to become full-fledged Engineers with BTech degree. There is also a problem for the BTech passed out students to get recognition of two years BTech module of NERIST after two years of Diploma in outside institutes and industries. All these problems need careful, sensible and intelligent solutions. For preserving the unique three module structure with vertical mobility and horizontal terminality, the following suggestions may be thought of:

(a) To devise a scheme to implement horizontal terminality on voluntary basis by the students. This is possible, at least to a certain extent, if massive and considerable campus recruitment is arranged for the Base Module passed out and Diploma Module passed out students at the sole and concerted initiatives of NERIST. It is also legitimate that passed out Base and Diploma holders should get adequate opportunity and encouraging avenues for terminality including respectable job prospects. At the same time there should be some options for the students opting out to go for higher studies after a minimum period of specific job experience, say Four years and Six years, respectively, in the NERIST system. The proposed measures will definitely be sources of attractions for voluntary terminality. The Masters Degree under type of NBE is surely as good as that of M.S. (online).

(b) The option for higher degrees for the students opting out at Base and Diploma may be created as in provision of type of examination called NBE (National Board of Examination) successfully operative in Medical Education. The students who opt out and are getting experience after Base and Diploma Level may appear NBE type examination to be judiciously framed and conducted by NERIST in order to make them earn Diploma and BTech Degree, respectively.

(c) Instead of issuing two years BTech degree after Diploma, it will be a reasonable suggestion to issue four years BTech certificate to the BTech passed out students scrapping the diploma certificate, after the students successfully complete the BTech programme.

3

Teaching Guidelines & Invocations

In order to achieve the desired goal of excellence and innovations in each and every function of National Institute of Technology–Arunachal Pradesh and to implement 'B' Plan in totality, I call upon my distinguished Members of Faculty to invest some of their valuable business time in doing Research on Teaching. In this context, I put forward the following general guidelines for teaching practices in the institute:

(i) J.C. Bose model of teaching: As an example, in the Basic Electronics course instead of first teaching the colour codes of the resistors in a theoretical class, teacher may carry few resistors to class and note down on the blackboard the colours of resistors and their values. Thereafter, the teacher may ask the students to devise the colour code creating enthusiasm among students. Similarly, instead of teaching the characteristics of P.N junction diode, teacher may guide the students in a laboratory to draw the characteristics curve they may advise the students to analyzse the behaviour of characteristics. Thereafter, the teacher may teach the theory of P.N junction diode.

(ii) S.N. Bose model of teaching: This is the conventional model of teaching where theory is first practiced; but even then, I suggest some unique ideas to improve imaginative power and creativity of students in the subject. For example, instead of teaching two algorithms for conversion of decimal to binary, one for integral part and another for fractional part, I call upon the teachers to design a single algorithm for both the purposes for inspiring teaching.

(iii) I also believe that a nobel teaching will be simple and in a simpler way. Therefore, I call upon the teachers not to teach bandpass filter, low-pass filter, highpass filter separately. Teachers may design a single circuit for all the filters and put on condition thereon can derive separately circuits for separate filters.

Similarly, instead of teaching RL, RC and RLC circuits separately, I call upon the teachers to teach only RLC circuit and then putting suitable condition on RLC circuit; RL and RC circuits may be derived and taught.

(iv) Last but not the least, I call upon the teachers to solve all the problems of all the chapters of the main text book prescribed for a subject in a teaching-learning process – 50 per cent to be solved by the teachers (may be bearing the even nos.) and 50 per cent may be solved by students (may be bearing the odd nos.).

I solicit and anticipate full cooperation from my brilliant pool of young and energetic faculty members to practice the nobel and novel teaching procedures explained above without fail. Once procedures implemented by the teachers are documented, we may proceed to file a patent on Research in Teaching on behalf of NIT - Arunachal Pradesh.

I propose a 'B' formula to achieve the primary goal of producing World Class Visionary Engineers and exceptionally brilliant Researchers and Innovators:

B-FORMULA

- Best for Teaching
- Best for Research
- Best for Entrepreneurship and Innovation
- Best for Services to Society

In implementing the 'B' formula in letter and spirit, the framing of syllabi should be taken as an important legitimate parameter. Therefore, extraordinary efforts and dedications need to be directed for to frame syllabus in a framework perhaps not available in the country as of today. Besides attention on 'B' formula, the Institute should give considerable importance to the major faults of current Technical Education while framing the syllabus. The major stumbling blocks in Technical Education today are:

(i) The present system is producing "Academic Engineers" rather than "Practical Engineers".

(ii) The present system of education makes the students to run after jobs rather than making them competent to create jobs.

(iii) There is lack of initiative to implement the reality of "Imagination is more important than knowledge".

Taking due consideration of the findings made above, to my mind a credible syllabus may be framed in which the major innovations as below may be introduced:

(i) I-course (Industrial Course) one in each semester at least one, which should be targeted to be taught by the Industrial expert at least upto 50 per cent of its component.

(ii) Man making and service to society oriented compulsory credit courses of NCC/ NSS, values and ethics, yoga etc.

(iii) Compulsory audit course on Entrepreneurship for all branches.

(iv) Many add-on courses those are (non-credit courses) to be offered in vacation to enhance the employability of the students.

(v) Many audit courses like French, German, Chinese to enhance the communication skill in global scale for the students.

(vi) Research and imagination building courses such as Research Paper Communication.

(vii) Design course as "Creative Design".

Further, the syllabus should be framed not to fit in a given structure as we believe structure is for syllabus and syllabus is not for structure. Therefore, as per requirement of the courses, the structure, the credit and the contact hours have to be made available in case to case basis.

The syllabus is also to be innovative when it includes:

(i) In addition to the list of text and reference books, a list of journals and magazines for giving students flexibility of open learning.

(ii) System of examination in each course as conventional examination, open book examination and online examination.

Each course should be framed with definite objectives and learning outcomes. The syllabus has also to be identified the courses to be taught either of two models of teaching:

(i) J.C. Bose model of teaching where practice is the first theory.

(ii) S.N. Bose model of teaching where theory is the first practice.

Besides, the a scheme of simple and best teaching in which, below example may be introduced:

(i) Instead of teaching RL, RC and RLC circuit separately, only RLC circuit will be taught and with given conditions on RLC circuits, RL and RC circuits will be derived and left to the students as interest-building exercise.

(ii) Instead of teaching separately High Pass filter, Band Pass filter and Low Pass filter etc; one circuit of filter will be taught to derive out other circuits, on conditions by the students.

4

ICT : A Design Tool of RTE

A few exceptional and credible achievements of the Central Government to my understanding are introduction of three Bills: RTE (Right to Education), RTI (Right to Information) and FSB (Food Security). The gap between people's expectations and Government's priorities may considerably be reduced by effective execution of these enactments. It is not that the Acts are without any scope of exploitations; but they are no doubt deliverable in nature. In fact, results or outputs of any initiative is of exact notion of 15 per cent Policy and 85 per cent implementation. Implementation needs creative design. It is noticed that implementation design for the enactments are badly lacking.

Restricting the discussion on RTE, it is deservely understood that effective design for executing RTE is undoubtedly easier, simpler and flexible with judicious, appropriate, selective and transparent (JAST) application of Information and Communication Technology (ICT). The major stumbling blocks of implementing RTE in letter and spirit are understood to be (i) bringing students (particularly in rural areas where parents believe that employing their children in labour market earns more money than sending them to school) to the schools, (ii) providing schools to rural students within comfortable coverage distance

(iii) non-availability of adequate number of teachers on ground of non-availability of quality and non-affordability by the Government on budgetary constraints (iv) non-availability of printed materials and books for imparting education.

Is ICT a tool to remove the barriers stated above for execution of RTE? Is therefore ICT is just a correct design for implementation of RTE? Let melook into the positiveness with a brief analysis.

ICT is a fantastic solution to provide learning and teaching in a most effective and so far unknown manner of flexibilities. ICT is all-time, all-location and all-form teacher in machine. It may provide teaching and learning at leisure period and in the night, as a available teacher at the door all the time. It duly meets the convenience of the rural students who often as desired by their parents opt for working in the day while skipping conventional school hours.

It is also desirable that for meaningful applications of RTE, schools should go to the students particularly in rural and poor areas rather than rural and poor community coming to the conventional geographical localised schools.

This essential desirability is uniquely met with applications of ICT design. The ICT availability of the peg at the door of the rural community surely removes the problem of going to schools located at the far away distance very often on bare foot. In ICT mode, teachers are logically in-built in the PCs (personal computers/laptops). The logical teacher teaches by virtue of animation which provides multimedia effects "See, Feel, Hear and Learn" in teaching. Such a fabulous teaching is highly effective, pretty inspiring and more attractive for the young children. ICT also resolves the issue of non-availability of the teachers and that of the printed materials for the purpose of learning.

It is a sad aspect, in our country that affordability (cost) and accessibility (electricity, communication link) will surely stand on the way of ICT design for execution of RTE in major parts of the rural areas. To tackle the problems, it will perhaps be not illogical and wrong to suggest that Government. at the selected rural areas in a cluster of few villages, may create a community centre of ICT. Such centre will have a few PCs, laptops with wireless connectivity and powered by solar power station.

Initially, such centres may finally and gradually go to each village, till affordability and accessibility are solved to a greater extent.

Core Social Research since ancient times is to find techniques and solutions either to remove or to reduce the gaps between haves and haves not. This gap is usually measured by a parameter called GNP/GDP. Unfortunately, the gap is neither being removed nor been reduced.

To reduce the gap between the human quality, so many research, so many initiatives have ever been undertaken in the world. Even then in terms of HDI, the countries in the world are sharply divided.

The scientific search aims for an ultimate answer to "What for we are here and why we are here". We are yet to arrive to a decisive answer.

Technology was developed for solving many problems people are facing in the world. Unfortunately, as of today most pertaining technology and most impact oriented technology known as Information Technology has classified the societies and the countries in the world in two groups namely: informal rich and informal poor. A fantastic concept being exercised in Bhutan is by measuring the peoples' expectation through "Happiness".

Perhaps the parameter of "Happiness" is something eternal that our religious Gurus and Philosophers thought of.

5

Brief Idea on Ranking of Indian Institutes

Raising the rank of Indian Universities and Institutes in World Ranking will decisively be a sound strategy for the nation to get a competitive advantages making Higher Technical Education Internationalised and globally acceptable to International students. Internationalised Indian Higher and Technical Education will not only promote our rich and solid achievement in education and culture but at the same time will enhance the National Economy and productivity. Even if there are unavoidable and reasonable questions on the existing systems of evaluation of rankings undertaken by different global agencies, yet then the high ranked Universities mostly are of developed countries. Thus, the correlation between education and economy is emphatically clear and loud. It is felt that magnifying the issue of faulty/biased ranking process to a large extent is getting to be something of a non-issue. Rather let us prepare ourselves in our own system of ranking or let us make us appropriate to reckon with in existing system. In the context, for making a good strategy for earning rank it is felt that Accredition process should be strengthened in a uniform manner and unidirectionally. Highly accredited

Universities and Institutes may then be put on in exercising to be in sound ranking endeavour globally.

It is a matter of great concern to many that the existing Accredition process in India has no uniformity neither is it a system of ours own. Copying a system under is definitely a debatable issue and not without questions. It is a rational thinking to devise our own system of evaluation for Accredition rather than being constantly copying the system of others.

The existing systems of Accredition in India today are:

(i) NAAC and (ii) NBA.

It is often argued that NAAC is primarily for Non-Technical Universities and NBA is for Engineering Universities/Colleges. Modern Education System definitely does not support the classification and draws boundary of Science, Humanities, Engineering and Technology. Clustering and interdisciplinary areas of study is the key to making today's Higher Education and Technical Education most fitting and deliverable. Therefore, having two types of a Accredition for today's boundary less clustering education is both meaningless and not a policy of thoughtful exercise. Further, it is often said that NBA is for Departmental-Wise/ Discipline-Wise accredition process whereas NAAC for overall Institutes. It seems most ridiculous if we think of an evaluation system we duly follow in giving a mark sheet to a student. When we issue mark sheet, we give grade for evaluation of each of the subjects and overall evaluation of the semester performance. Therefore, if we assume subject paper is a discipline and semester is the Institute, where is the wrong in having a uniform and one accredition process?

There has emerged an emphatic need to integrate NAAC and NBA; and to make integrated accredition process mandatory for all Institutes/Universities taking part in global ranking under existing agencies undertaking the evaluation for ranking.

Without being always a follower, India should also attempt to be a leader in devising a credible process of accredition and ranking of the Institutes and Universities. Copying the process adopted by others may neither be appropriate nor be a judicious one for our country on the long run.

Most of the accredition proceses and ranking systems now operative globally are found to be fundamentally based on inputs and outputs. Any ranking or accredition is by the parameters of inputs and outputs, although these being undoubtedly major parameters to reckon with, will not be correct one. A system generating better and higher outputs with lower inputs is always superior to a system generating substantial output with maximum input. Therefore, accredition and ranking should be based on the productivity defined as:

Productivity = output ÷ input

Productivity in different units may be measured and normalised to have a process of accredition and ranking. For example a few productivity measurements may be estimated as below:

i. *Productivity of Research* may be measured as (average number of publications in SCI journals per faculty member + average number of patent per faculty member) ÷ the Research expenditure in a particular year.

ii. *Productivity of students'* performance may be measured as average grade (Result) of outgoing students ÷ average rank of the same students admitted, (Rank may be Rank of Joint Entrance Examination).

iii. *Teaching productivity* may be Teachers-students ratio.

iv. *Teachers Quality Productivity* = No. of PhD holders ÷ Total no. of Teachers

Similarly, the innovation productivity, the investment productivity, the students employability productivity, the industrial linkage productivity etc., may be defined and estimated. The idea proposed may be deliberated upon in wider and higher platforms to arrive at a conclusive decision.

6

Redesigning Higher Technical Education to meet National Aspirations

Currently in the process of imparting technical education in India there are basically two layers of systems: Prestigious Institutes of National Importance (IITs / NITs) and AICTE approved institutes. Some thoughts are suggested for possible improvement of technical education in different systems. Liberalisation, Globalisation and Privatisation to which India participated in 1992 has opened up great challenges, viabilities and potentialities subject to adoption and changes. Generation of a deliverable brilliant pool of national human resource is decisively a sound strategy for any developing country for competitive advantage in the current globalised economy. Economy and Education are most important for any country, and these are dependent on each other, not replacement. Today like never before, national development is closely related to the application of science and technology in the developmental process. The wisdom of being developed is therefore how exceptionally finest is the national intelligent resource and how closely generation system of human resources fits the national requirement. India despite claiming to be the third largest technical manpower in the world, has not yielded the expected results. This calls for reviewing of current technical education system of India towards devising a mechanism for result oriented transformation keeping in mind return on investment made by the country.

The current technical education in India is objectively structured, of course not limited to, just producing, in general "academic engineers" rather than "technical engineers" and in generating engineers who in general run after jobs rather than building minds to create at least certain jobs. What is strongly, quickly and massively needed is surely a changed, innovative and country specific model; (not necessarily following the developed countries' models always), of technical education system as a whole. Innovations are the need of the hour in regard to framing syllabus to meet the aspirations of applying products of the system to build developed India. The emphasis requires to be done on the spirits of "practice is the first theory" in teaching, "credit and time structure is for content and content is not for structure, ie., not fixing content of any course in a time bound structure".

In designing the contents of any subject paper, "giving higher emphasis in thinking and imagination process over dissemination process" in teaching mechanism, "do while learning" in environment, "entrepreneurship teaching" as essentiality, "human values, ethics, NCC and NSS" for holistic man making, and finally changing the evaluation process from current practice on "how much you do not know" to "how much you know." The introduction of on line examination both for objective and subjective evaluation and open book examination will be rational in this context.

Creation of technical or practical engineers calls for one way rethinking on radical change of establishing laboratories in the institutes and in another way revising institute industry interaction. For a long period these exercises of institute industry interaction have not made any note worthy impact. It is suggested that as and where the interaction is essential, there is no reason as to why institutes will not establish in some of the selected laboratories, small industries. Industries of institutes will certainly create an in built institute industry interaction never thought of before. As teachers do consultancy for industries and as the laboratory product is the first and foremost for commercial production, the proposal of industry by institute is duly feasible and definitely realisable. What is needed is a changed mindset for acceptance. Further such a proposal may create huge IRG (Internal Resource Generation) for which each institute is working for. In private sector, if the proposal is allowed and accepted, it is supposed to bring revolution in industrial infrastructure in the country. It is absolutely necessary to think of a model fitting the need of the country. What is doing very good in one country may be disaster for another country. This is how the mind set is needed to be changed.

Country is in crying need of adequate number of quality teachers. Dedicated resourceful teachers having crunch thrust for learning and spontaneous zeal for research, as quality higher education is imbridged with research, are pillars of any extraordinary institutes. Practice of several measures exercised by this time for attracting teaching profession has not produced desired results.

The practices in this regard undertaken so far are found to focus on offered enhanced and extra financial packages. The measures on financial gains may create certainly not an environment of getting teachers "by choice." There is a need for creating conducive environment and culture for attracting bright and scholastic students to opt for teaching by choice. Generating interest in teaching at early stage may be thought of. The students by merit of 4th year of B Tech classes may be given some opportunity to teach in 2nd year classes for generating teaching and research interest among finest young minds besides existing financial packages and facilitate in house off the peg availability of PG course and PhD programme. This kind of environment may bring a cultural mind change for fruitful availability of teachers by choice.

Barrier-free, less-rule based and liberal-grant based research culture should be another goal of any prospective institute for competitive survival and sustainable growth. In house research and PhD programme for both young teachers and students should emphatically be encouraged and enhanced if required with innovative practices of quality control. Now-a-days some not-to-be-dismissed suspicious about in house PhD for internal teachers are reported. Such issues need innovative measures to curb with rather than killing the legacy of historically established research foundation in any institute. What is suggested that the submitted thesis of one Institute (parent) may be sent to another Institute (foreign) for evaluation. The foreign Institute will be responsible for finding experts for evaluation of thesis, and once the evaluation reports are received, the reports will be sent to the parent Institute for the acceptance or rejection as per prevailing rules.

Last but not the least the assessment of institutes if is done by the quality of products only they produce it may not serve the right national purpose. More meaningful and appropriate parameter for assessment of institutes should be productivity defined as ouput divided by input. What is output for a given input is decisively more important than what is just the output. The national assessment process to some extent will be wrong if simply copied from other countries, and may like to seriously look into measuring the productivity of the institutes for grading institutes among others things.

Innovations and applications of art of novelty are of paramount importance to exercise the importance of making students who will eventually be made to accept "what you do with what you know is more important than what you know" and "Imagination is more important than knowledge." Institutes should be made for Innovation, Expansion and Excellency with autonomy as far as practicable, being independent in full and thinking neither superior nor inferior to any other institute, and finally producing students as good as others if not superior.

The witness of growth of AICTE approved institutes needs a review. India is indeed a youth country in the world. Present population comprises about 55 per cent of youth of age of around 25. To meet the career aspiration of the vast youth population, the role of private investment in higher education is predominantly credible. Particularly in the last two decades, the growth, often described as a mushroom growth of private institutes all over the country is phenomenal, yet in general a matter of concern. The matters of concern mostly and primarily are quality, sustainability and reliability of the institutes and of the education the institutes impart Surely, there are certain private institutes of higher learning which by their own right and function are beyond the purview of these concerns.

In a statue of one of the highly established and top ranking Universities in India it is stated that the Vice Chancellor is the University. Reading not between the letters, but the spirit in between, it is an intangible inference that the academic leadership in any institute is the key. It is very important for any institute for the essential purpose of quality, sustainability and reliability to appoint and allow to function a Head of any institute as real Head rather than just a titoba Head or rubber stamp. Regulatories authorities have thus to play a key role in establishing or restoring as the case may be to realise this simple requirement of successful and result oriented system of higher education in the nation. It is imperative that the merit of private institutes will determine the level of intelligent resource and capability of the country in days to come as in number private institutes outplay the governmental institutes. Parallely for the sake of their sheer benefits, the private players should bend their heart and mind for accepting any feasible policy undertaken by the regulators in this direction.

Profit or return on investment should not be misunderstood and undermined in the private investment in higher education. The issue is most common and natural theory of flow of private investment in form of any establishment. Today after all, education is just not a service provider, but a service with customer satisfaction too. This necessarily means that any policy framed to achieve desired ouputs should not dilute the fundamental scope of investment, i.e., some profit. The fundamental parameters of achieving quality, sustainability and reliability of higher educational institutes are qualified and dynamic (not either of) Director/Vice Chancellor, reckoning academic infrastructure and brilliant pool of faculty members. It will not be so inappropriate if the selection of Director/Vice Chancellor is regularised by a process abridged with approval process. As an example, AICTE/UGC may prepare a list of potential Directors/Vice Chancellors, may be either State wise meeting the requirement and sentiment of state or Nation-wise. Private managements have to appoint Director/Vice Chancellor from the list. Such appointment by the private management may not necessarily be on merit order in the list that will provide them due flexibility on selection from the fitting pool of candidates. Remaining two parameters require to be controlled in letter and spirit and full independently by Head of the institute, Director or Vice chancellor. At the same time requirement for these parameters is money. It calls for thus according a part and substantial financial power to Directors/Vice Chancellors of private institutes. There is no reason not to link a procedure of delegation of financial power to Head of private institutes in the approval process without diluting the fundamental theory of investment. A suggestion may be that at least 33 per cent (one third/ may be otherwise worked out appropriately) of yearly earned tution fees will be under the control of Head of each private institute purely for the purpose of expenditure for the development of laboratories, library and the salaries and perks of members of faculty. Other required developmental issues and recurring costs will be the sole discretion of the management. The procedure may be chalked out accordingly to incorporate the same in the approval process. It is further categorically needed that before implementation of the ideas or related ideas, wide deliberations may be imitated for arriving at a definite conclusion. There is nothing wrong accepting regulations for good cause and long turn benefits, rather sticking to mathematical regulations.

Today's trend of education is largely aimed at managing jobs. The trend has brought the so far known economic theory of demand and supply in technical higher education sector. Primarily due to overall poor job market in engineering sector over the last few years, there has been noticed a gradual fall in admission rate in private institutes. There has thus emerged a need of taking some innovative and leadership action to meet with the alarming situation arisen out of very low admission putting at stake the mere survival of some of the institutes. It should be clearly and squarely understood that private institutes on natural rule of investment cannot be expected to run for a long time with minimal enrollment. In the context, AICTE may take a leading role in allowing private technical institutes to run BA, BSc, BCom MA, MCom, MSc and allied courses concurrently with due understanding of approved way with other regulators including affiliating universities and the state governments.

7

Pioneer Innovations in Technical Education in Arunachal

The month of January is exceptionally rewarding for India. On this auspicious month India gave birth to a pool of legendaries like Swami Vivekananda, Dr S.N. Bose and Netaji Subhash Chandra Bose. Equally important is 26th January, the day India became a Republic. In the true sense therefore, January is significantly rising month for India for any year.

In this auspicious month of January let me highlight true spirit of rising sun of Arunachal Pradesh in India. Education is fast and foremost for any country for equitable and expansive growth and prosperity. Even in the history of world, no country has ever become developed without a brilliant pool of human resources and highest order of intellectual capabilities. With the advent of modern technology, in general and Information Technology, in particular fostering so fast and vast, the Technical Education has become utmost pillar for development of a Nation. In fact a nobel winning physicist told that the real difference between the developed and the developing is nothing but the application of Science and Technology. In summary therefore India needs to develop a highly qualitative, innovative, meaningful and expansive Technical Education system to become a centre of power in the world.

I firmly, fairly and strongly am of the opinion that for emphatic development of the Nation, its education system must not be and should not be a copied or a mixture of copied systems of other countries. We must keep in mind that we are basically labour intensive country and not a capital intensive country. Our education system must be therefore our country specific and relevant to the aspirations and needs of the country.

Since, the days of considerable attention and investment made by the Governments and in recent past by private sectors in the Technical Education system, to my mind, no fruitful innovation of any magnitude has ever been exercised in the Technical Education system. In the context Arunachal Pradesh is a proud initiator. Here I talk of ever being first innovation in Technical Education system in the Project of North Eastern Regional Institute of Science and Technology (NERIST) in 1986. As of today we often hear of inclusive growth, inclusive economy and inclusive development that cater from micro to macro level. The inclusive coverage has the beneficial effects and outputs. Inclusiveness ensures innovations and cost effective system. NERIST in the history of Technical Education in India was established on a modular Technical Education system that is logically a system of inclusive Technical Education catering Base, Diploma and UG Degree in a cluster. The innovations inbuilt in NERIST is a road map of high skilled generating and cost effective Technical Education system so appropriate, so justified and so appealing for a developing country like India. The road map created and practiced in NERIST got later transpired in another Institute known as SantLongwal Institute of Technology in Punjab.

It is not the question of whether the stated innovations started in Arunachal Pradesh have been preserved in totality but more importantly it is a fact that it created an example and historical document for the others to follow and entire country to remember. Logical and innovative solutions however may be thought of to preserve the innovations without anyway hampering the students' interest and aspiration in anyway but Arunachal Pradesh ought to claim the distinction of being the pioneer leader in starting the innovations.

In 2010, the Govt. of India took an extraordinary drive to strengthen Technical Education in the country by establishing one NIT (National Institute of Technology – Institute of National Importance (University) in each of the eight North Eastern states. NIT, Arunachal Pradesh is one of this brilliant exercise initiated by Govt. of India. The NIT family of Arunachal Pradesh has from its day of effective independent functioning introduced enormous innovations in Technical Education system which in certain cases is first ever in the whole of India. Such innovations are based on clear and fair understanding of the major lacuna of the existing Technical Education system. These are:

(i) Present system of Technical Education creates in general Academic Engineers rather than Technical Engineers.

(ii) Present system of Technical Education creates Engineers basically who do not create jobs rather than look for jobs.

(iii) In present Technical Education system there is hardly an attempt to generate nobel human mind with ethics and culture in-built and emphasize towards service to society.

(iv) Present Technical Education system is fundamentally a system of memorising documented knowledge rather than igniting thinking process and to exercise knowledge creation by realisation among students.

To address the stated major concerns of the Technical Education system, NIT, Arunachal Pradesh has boldly introduced various novelties a few of which are:

(i) Compulsory subject papers of NCC/NSS, values and ethics as man making exercise.

(ii) Compulsory subject papers on Entrepreneurship practice for inspiring Engineers towards Entrepreneurship and creation of jobs.

(iii) Compulsory subject papers of Research Paper communications for enhancing thinking process.

(iv) For the first time in the history of India NIT has started MTech in Appropriate Technology and Entrepreneurship in collaboration with National Institute of Rural Development (NIRD), Hyderabad.

(v) To offer more importance and values to "Evaluate to know how much students' know rather than how much they do not know", students' examination system has been made open book, online and on a flexible scaling.

NIT and NERIST are the symbols to its logical conclusion of innovations in Technical Education system in India. Both the institutes are in Arunachal Pradesh and therefore judiciously and by the right claim for the Rise jointly in the field of Technical Education in the 'Land of Rising Sun' in India.

8

Some Thoughts on making West Bengal a Leader in Technical Education

West Bengal was at the centre of education in the country during the days of independence. Unfortunately today it is not but at the same time definitely not at lowest. Time is ripe for recovery and repairing. Economy and education are so closely related that many credible studies have suggested to the all developing countries to accord top priority on generation of quality human resource for competitive advantages in the globalised world. Therefore most importantly and quickly, West Bengal needs to frame strategy and clear agenda for transformation to become a leader in education. In the exercise the picture of technical education in West Bengal requires prioritised review.

Establishing and operating higher technical educational institutes at the level of colleges and universities is undoubtedly Costly proposition. Therefore affordability of doing the same all by the state government alone in the required scale in a highly populated state is neither feasible nor expected. That is how perhaps West Bengal took more than three decades to establish another government engineering college after Jalpaiguri Government Engineering College. As a consequence the private investment in technical higher education is a welcome move and quite inevitable. As of today West Bengal is having around 50 Private Higher Technical institutes to cater to engineering education. Without any sort of any as persion on any such institute and purely for the sake of quality, sustainability and reliability (which are interdependant and essential) of these institutes, some suggestions are given for possible consideration and adoption to ensure West Bengal gets back its glorious position in the field of education in the country.

Historically leaders are not followers. Leaders may at best consider the experience of others but devise their own policies to win over others. It will be our sincere effort to see that West Bengal becomes an absolute leader in education to reckon with. Unfortunately in the name of centralised control of the private engineering institutes under one umbrella West Bengal has clearly copied the idea of establishing a State Bengal University of Technology, and the move is apparently copied from other states running private colleges since long. Such centralised control takes away the academic competition so important for improving and preserving quality. It is however not just that the State Technical University is lacking in pursuit of excellence. The mute issue raised is the academic competition for better quality. Had the private colleges been put under different universities (including State University of Technology) in clusters and within territorial jurisdiction of different universities, various colleges would have been under different course syllabus, various different academic regulations and administrative control as well providing location advantage. Due to healthy inherent academic autonomy of Universities, there would have been academic competition leading to achieving higher level of quality. Taking effective role in constructive competition is the only mechanism for achieving results in the ever changing and vibrant era. Quality guarantees durability and reliability to a great extent.

Today's trend of education is largely aimed at job performence. The trend has brought the so far known economic theory of demand and supply in technical higher education sector. Primarily due to an overall poor job market in the engineering sector over the last few years, there has been noticed a gradual fall in admission rate in private institutes. There has thus emerged a need of taking some innovative and leadership action to meet with the alarming situation arisen out of very low admission putting at stake the mere survival of some of the institutes. It should be clearly and squarely understood that private institutes on natural rule of investment cannot be expected to run for a long time with minimal enrolmemt. In the context, West Bengal may take a leading role in allowing private technical institutes to run BA, BSc, BCom, MA, MCom, MSc and allied courses concurrently with due understanding with regulators including All India Council for Technical Education. West Bengal may also take a role to aggressively open and market the educational opportunities in countries of Africa, Bhutan, Bangladesh, Nepal etc possibly by a consolidated approach to be undertaken by a consortium of state and private managements.

Resource sharing among private institutes may also be thought of. Sharing of the Buildings, Libraries and laboratories is out of purview in this context as it will create immense difficulties for the students. One of the hefty costly component in private institutes, basically after last pay revision is the salary of faculty members. To manage the situation a particular faculty member, subject to his or her sole voluntary consent, may be shared by two institutes preferably in nearby institutes. In one institute service may be rendered for three days a week and in another two days a week to serve academic assignment on a relatively higher load. This will result in sharing salary by the two institutes to the extent in providing full payable salary to the teacher, and will meet interest of both the institutes and the faculty member. Regulation should target the required objective not the mathematics. It is more important to examine "how and what is taught" rather than "how many have taught."

9

Excellency and Autonomy

Excellency and Autonomy (EA) are two sides of a coin when applied in higher education. They enrich each other. EA ought to be exercised in flexible, changeable and tolerable system of governance. There is no place of rigid and so called mathematical, copied and colonial rules in EA. Rules are for Institutes and Institutes are not for rules; and change is the only perpetual thing in the whole of universe. Our Mindset needs to be framed in rational and honest system of Institutional mechanism for the correct and right spirit of EA.

During the days of Nalanda University, India was at the Centre of Education in the world. Excellency had been there in the blood of Indian Higher Education. The then education was inherently and completely autonomous and under control and supervision and superintendence of only Gurujis – the academicians of higher order. Therefore, most appropriately before attempting to bring excellency in Indian Higher Education, there is a rational need to examine the reasons for sleeping out of the door of excellency over time. In fact, the education in India has not made the expected level in excellency because of not having inclusive definition of Excellency, and adherence to autonomy in practicality.

Education and economy are inclusive and interdependent. Attempting to make education excellent without due considerations to economy will be an exercise of complete futility. It is said that deliverable education enhances economic productivity which in turn acts as a feedback and feeder for academic excellence. Over the years, excellence earned in our Viswavidyalayas got wiped out because of subsequently not having attempted to make Education and Research as an integral part of delivery system of growth and productivity. Rather education was treated as a cost centre. Besides, inertia against accepting the changes or delay in exercising changes in education system necessarily are the stumbling blocks for not achieving excellence. Both making education deliverable and making education more with time are the two fundamental issues of achieving excellence. This necessarily needs changed mindset. At the same time, excellence can never be achieved by copying any system from developed countries. It is good to think globally and act locally, but not a good thing to think and act globally. Matching, feeling, appropriate, rational and country specific educations is what is required for achieving excellence.

Therefore, we need to look at the issue of achieving excellence in proper perspective, in holistical approach and in perspective of the country.

Autonomy without accountability is disaster. At the same time autonomy with authority is the prime drive of achieving excellence. Fact remains that changing mindset to deliver autonomy and accept autonomy is the need of time, basic of which will be "Be a leader not a copier". India had Nalanda because it was built on leadership not on copy-mastership. Autonomy must be clearly understood in this spirit and exercised accordingly. Irrational beliefs that copying what the so called globally high ranked universities are doing will make us reach the milestone is a major stumbling block for achieving autonomy. What we cannot do, if we do not do is not a crime; but what we can do if we do not do is a crime.

Autonomy in hand of good man yields results, but in hand of bad man may be disaster. Therefore, autonomy needs to be given only when a deserving leader is identified and appointed. Appropriate person may only be meaningfully apply autonomy in true spirit and practice of:

A: Authority with command and confidence. Leader is expected to exercise for what is best in his/her opinion for the Universities/Institutes.

U : Untiring efforts to stop Unitary Practice of Rules and Regulations as needed for result-oriented action in any Universities/Institute. In name of autonomy, practice of applying pre-framed rules and criteria in all Central Institutes/Universities is neither autonomy nor any way good for anything. Practicising rules and regulations so appropriate for Institutes in Delhi may be so much inappropriate for Institutes in Arunachal Pradesh.

T : Technically feasible solution only be understood by the leader before application.

O : Openness to accept changes for opportunities.

N : "No" to rules imposed by supporting authority whereas rules are not for good of the Institute. Rules are for Institutes and Institutes are not for rules.

O : Overcome difficulties and not referring to sponsoring agency and convert difficulties into opportunities.

M : Monotony and Monopoly should be avoided.

Y : Say always "Yes" to changes with time for making autonomy meaningful and deliverable.

Two issues/examples are sighted below to explain how autonomy and excellence are facing problems for so called Rules:

Example: 1. Administrative Rule:

The requirement of Members of Faculty in Universities/ Institutes is usually based on a sanction accorded by Teacher-Students' ratio. For example in NITs the ratio is 1:12 whereas in IITs it is 1:10. The calculation for creation of Members of Faculty based on the parameter of Teacher-Students' ratio is found to be irrational and illogical on several aspects. If the requirement is calculated based on total strength of the students' in any Institute or University, the requirement becomes unjustified on several accounts. For example, the issues of two Institutes NITs 'A' and 'B' may be compared. Institute 'A' is having say 3 Departments having intake of 40 per Department for Four Years courses. Therefore, the Institute 'A' is entitled to get a sanction of Total Faculty of (40 intake x 4 years duration of course x 3 No. of Departments = 480 ÷ 12) 40. This means each of the 3 Departments of Institute 'A' will have a total faculty strength of (48 ÷ 3) 16.

Let Institute 'B' having 4 Departments each with 30 intakes. Therefore, as per existing policy, the Institute is to have (30 x 4 x 4 = 480 ÷ 12) = 48 Members of Faculty. Therefore, in this Institute each Department will get 48 ÷ 4) 12 Members of Faculty. So, if we compare the Institute 'A' and 'B' we find where Institute 'A' is having 16 Faculty Members per Department. Institute 'B' is only having 12 Faculty Members per Department. That shows a gross injustice to the Institute 'B'.

Example: 2. Academic Rules:

Indian Nobel Winners and Great Scientists studied in the then system of curriculum where there was (i) no fixed maximum or minimum credit has to be convered in a Semester/Course; (ii) no fixed maximum or minimum number of subject papers to be covered etc and etc. Again we find Rule is made for Rule and not as per the requirement of any subject paper or course work. This is how we are slipping from excellence.

Autonomy is needed for Directors/Vice-Chancellors to overrule Rules for actually meeting the purpose and objectives and NOT the Rules for the sake of Rules.

10

Making New India with Transformed Education

Nelson Mandela, a great philosopher and world leader said, *"Education is a powerful weapon which you can use to change the world"*. This is how Education is first, economy next. This is why economy is the most important for any country, not missile. And that is why there is an essentiality to design "Education" as a deliverable system specific to a country's aspiration, expectation and needs. For a highly populated, agricultural based and labour intensive country, a rational technical education system is there in what Swami Vivekananda said *"Educate people technically, morally and intellectually and support self-sufficiency and service to others"*, read with Mahatma Gandhi's philosophy of development of the country as he said, *"The True India is to be found not in the few cities, but in its seven hundred thousand villages. If the villages perish, India will perish too."*

In the context of educating people technologically and making it relevant and deliverable system for the development of true New India, several paramount issues need to be carefully resolved out of which a few important issues with due corrective suggestions are:

(1) Judicious Selection of the Technological Disciplines with due priorities and Rightful framing of appropriate syllabus. Giving importance to competency in system design and application rather than competency only in (and particular with more emphasis in) theory and memorised education. This is for making education deliverable. Several noteworthy suggestions in this context will be:

(a) Courses of Appropriate Technology like interdisciplinary subjects, Agriculture Technology, Farming Technology, Bamboo Technology, Tea Technology, Fisheries, Horticulture, Housing Technology, Hosiery Technology and mother engineering like Mechanical Engineering, Chemical Engineering, Civil Engineering and relevant frontier technology like Bio and Mechanical Technology as full fledged 4-Years BTech Programme with priority and strict directive and monitoring that such courses are not for job seekers but for job creators for which Govt. should liberally sponsor such courses in the means of free education and grant of sufficient soft loan as an obligation for promoting job creation at the end of 4-Years studies. Priorities need to be pushed rather than only framed. Yes we need teachings like computing, micro-electronics, mobile computing etc., but those should be operated in the conventional mode and with some boundary conditions so that the software coolies are not abundantly produced in India making it a cheap labour supplier to the developed countries and Engineers do not become a factory product of unemployed human factory.

(b) Because of our motto so far of being follower rather than leader, the concept of making syllabus of a fixed credit of fixed contact hours is not only ridiculous but also unproductive. Many exceptional and brillian students had been produced by India with the courses which had no boundary conditions. It is suggested that course structure and syllabus must be framed as required for meeting the coverage of the course without having any condition therein. This forward looking step is essential to produce exceptional Engineers like that of J.C. Bose, Visyeswaraya among others.

(c) To make educational system deliverable and innovative there is a need to impart Entrepreneurship Education at every branch of Engineering and Technology as mandatory.

(d) For making innovations a practice of teaching and learning, it is imperative that the examination system should be radically revamped and framed. It is required to examine "How far a student does know", and not "How far a student does not know". Similarly, investigative knowledge and chance for giving importance to investigative knowledge" over memorised knowledge is the need of the time. In this context open-book examination system, on-line examination system must overtake the conventional exam system. It further should be allowed if examination system is selectively made operative where all students in a class will set questions and class teacher will pick up question for examination from the question-bank prepared by students.

(e) To make education thought provoking, it will be necessary to introduce compulsory courses like "Research Paper Communication" and "Creative System Design". In such subject papers at least 50 per cent of the content may be of self-study based on which students on rotation may be asked to deliver compulsory lecture in full class in presence of class teacher.

(f) Alongwith quality education, substantial attention is imperative for making students "Mentally sound and physically fit" for which compulsory subject papers on

"NCC/NSS" and "Values and Ethics" should be included in syllabus.

(g) Besides enabling environment for Entrepreneurship promotion; opportunities need to be made for making our students globally employable for which there should be due provision in syllabus for optional training in skill generation in global languages of English, Chinese, Korean, German, French etc, alongwith add-on courses on PHP, Ruby etc.

(2) Meticulous efforts are the need of the time in making education applicable, appropriate and achievable. In an enormous and splendid thought provoking article "Learning from one Author", The Hindu, January 14, 2014, Nobel Winning Economist Dr Amartya Sen said *"The Skill of doing research, the hard preparation needed for doing new and original work – going beyond the old established knowledge, and indeed the courage to think in novel and daring lines – are all immensely helped by good and exciting teaching"*. Teaching needs urgent revamping", *Teaching should not be just dissemination of documented knowledge in books and papers. Teaching should be delivered with art, philosophy and imagination. Rather than teaching* 2+2 = 4, *it is more inspiring to teach why* 2+2 *is not equal to say* 5 *but* 4?

(3) Teaching Methodology particularly in technical education requires instant innovation. It is hard to logically, rationally and judiciously believe that all subject papers in engineering education be taught in one way/conventional way of theory first and practice next. Teaching may primarily be made in two modes:

(a) J.C. Bose model in which philosophy will be "Practice is the first theory". To name a few subjects that are fitting to this mode are *"Programming in C", "Circuits and Theory", "Engineering Drawing", "Workshop Practice" etc.*

(b) S.N. Bose model in which practice and philosophy will be "Theory is the first practice" as in present conventional mode of teaching.

(4) Practice of Green and Clean Campus and Environment is prominently desirable.

Making New India is important and so is of Transforming Education in equitable scope. Task is tough, Road is Long. Hope for the best to reach it soon.

11

Making New India with New Education

Essentiality of Quality Teaching and Research for making New India is undoubtedly understood by each and everyone. A careful examination of the reasons for not having desired quality teaching and research in Higher Technical Educational Establishments in India reveals the followings:

- Severe shortage of not just number of Members of Faculty but essentially shortage of dedicated and quality and innovative Members of Faculty is alarming. In the present scenario, it is hard but true to say that in general the teaching profession is full of "Teachers by chance" (sometimes some persons perhaps correctly call them as residuals) rather than "Teachers by choice". Time is ripe to arrest the increasing gap between "Teachers by choice" and "Teachers by chance"
- It is also a fact that all "Teachers by chance" are not second to all "Teachers by choice", but in general there is an emergent need to have more and more "Teachers by choice" in our educational establishments.
- It is very sad that no innovation has ever been exercised and undertaken to make teaching attractive, investigative, thought-provoking and philosophical so deserving for

sheer benefits of learners. We accustomed to copied system of teaching which is just delivery of documented knowledge with ever increasing competition of colourful presentation only; and this has got a name of ICT based delivery. It must be understood that human brains are ever fertile to challenge of the ICT based fixed delivery.

- The age old practice of India that gave birth to luminaries like C.V. Raman, S.N. Bose, M. N. Saha, J.C. Bose among others of synergic and integrated practice of teaching and research has been duly forgotten and not in force in general in the Institutes of higher learning. "Teaching with Research" and "Research with Teaching" are badly missing from the culture, practice, preaching and promotion in Indian Institutes. Professionalism has how taken back seat and career is taking over.
- The age old practice or copied practice of recruiting Members of Faculty in a process the recruitment is made in offices has measurably failed to really select the geniuses for teaching in Higher Educational Establishments.

To address the issues a few proposals may be thought of:

1. There is a need to introduce a five point RQA (Recruitment & Quality Assurance) Scheme for recruitment of dedicated and qualitative teachers in the educational establishments as stated below:

   i. Each Institute should have a Career counseling team made of Eminent Professors to counsel the bright students to opt for teaching as a profession with guidance of novelty, flexibility and prosperity available in the teaching profession.

   ii. Teachers should not be recruited the way recruitment is made for offices. There is an urgent need for search for deserving teachers for which Directors must be empowered to search potential candidates and employ them with subsequent reporting to BoG (Board of Governance) giving credible justification of the candidates so searched and appointed.

iii. It is felt that all initiatives till date for attracting bright students in teaching profession are focused on giving more money and better perks. There is no attempt to generate interest among the students in the teaching profession. Leading Institutes may introduce the scheme of engaging bright students of Final Year BTech and MTech to teach in lower classes with a token honorarium of say Rs 500 for one hour theory classes or three hours practical classes.

iv. Recruitment of teachers with just PhD needs to be modified. We must recruit teachers with PhD as minimum and at least with three published papers in the referred journals to ensure the quality of the PhD. Otherwise, to meet the minimum only PhD requirement, the quality of PhD will get diluted.

v. The process of teaching by recruited teachers will be qualitative and technically befitting if teachers' confirmation is made only when teachers in grade of Assistant Professors take at least two Industrial Training in the summer vacations at full sponsorship of the Institute.

2. Some proposals are given below for making teaching attractive and meaningful:

i. Subject papers in syllabus of the technical courses must be taught in two models. Proposed models are J.C. Bose model where "practice will be the first theory" and S.N. Bose model where "theory will be the first practice". There is no meaning of teaching 'C' programming in lecture classes as there is no such meaning to starting teaching mathematics in practice classes.

ii. Teaching must not be just delivery of the documented knowledge. It should be thought provoking for which teaching with research should be made a Rule in the Institutes. There is no reason why just teaching "how 2 + 2 = 4" may not be discouraged as there is no reason why it should not be encourage to teach that "why 2 + 2 is not equal to 5". A perfect combination of "why" and "how" in teaching must be promoted in the Institutes. Innovating teaching must be exercised as a Rule, as an example of which will be not to teach RL, RC circuits but to teach RLC circuit only and thereafter putting necessary conditions to teach RL and RC circuits.

iii. Teaching must be supplemented with value addition and making students mentally fit and physically sound for which adequate numbers of NCC/NSS and value added courses should be added in the curriculum.

iv. To innovate the process of examination, question banks prepared by teachers and students may be used selectively and suitably for Technical Education.

v. Design Contest and research paper communication may be made compulsory for mind-blowing and thought-provoking exercise.

For taking leadership in Higher Technical Education in this world today, investment and innovation are of paramount importance. Investment in Higher Education in framework of economy of the country is reasonably understood but what is not understood is the reasons for absence of drives to make paradigm shifts in Higher Technical Education by academic leaders. Important shifts are changing mindset from just quality to quality + innovation, from just publication to publication + production (deliverable and impact oriented Research), from just teaching to teaching + learning, from just job giving and seeking to job creating and from just knowledge to knowledge + values and ethics. It may not be wrong to say that the shifts to make NEW INDIA may fail, if we do not change culture from experts to innovators/thinkers in shaping Indian Education.

12

Choice Based Credit System : Some thoughts

Attempt to introduce choice based credit system in Higher Education is being propagated. Every system has pros & cons. India has a bad legacy particularly in higher education to be followed. Copying what is found to be a good system in other countries without merit analysis of the same in the context of Indian environment and requirements may be an exercise in complete futility in India. At the same time, outright rejection of any idea put forward is never a nice thing. Therefore, before acceptance or rejection of choice based credit system a sincere and credible examination of the system towards promotion is reasonably, legitimately and logically required, in the context of which a SWOT analysis is done as follows:

- **Strengths:**

Choice Based Credit System (CBCS) is a stakeholder – friendly particularly for the students. It is reasonably student–centric in place of existing system that is to a extent teacher-centric.

➢ CBCS is inherently a flexible and adoptable system. Flexibility in terms of choice of subject papers is guaranteed. Adaptability for suiting a student's personal choice is paramountly omnipresent in the system.

- Wide scope of expertise in different areas may be created in any Institute to meet the choices of students under CBCS, making the Institute rich in infrastructure.
- There is a growing trend towards CBCS.

- **Weakness:**

Operational difficulty in the Institute located in remote and disadvantageous areas may not cater to the requirement of choices of CBCS.

- Till now there is no guaranteed evidence of CBCS being superior to fixed credit system. India has produced great luminaries like Viseswaraya, Dr. C.V. Raman, Dr. S.N. Bose, Dr. M.N. Saha among others in fixed structure credit system.
- While there is an acute shortage of Members of Faculty all over the country, the requirement of more teachers to meet mere and various choices in quality application of teaching in the CBCS is necessarily a weak area.

- **Opportunities:**

The current world scenario of liberalization, privatization and globalization demands a pool of versatile skilled human resources like IT persons with knowledge of accounting, Mechanical Engineers with knowledge of Electronics etc. CBCS will necessarily be an opportunity to create the stated, thos demanding versatile skilled manpower in new order of business and industry.

- The pressure originating from non-liked courses in a fixed system sometimes becomes the source of destruction for the students and sometimes mentally upset students leading to suicides. In CBCS such situations are expected to demolish.

- **Threats:**

Due to choice offered to the students (particularly for immature students) may lead to producing semi-skilled/half-skilled labours dangerously non-productive for any society. Students may also be prompted to choose high-scoring subjects that may not necessarily be of competency building.

> ➢ Choices may lead to prompt the students to opt for only short run job oriented courses rather than core competency courses required and expected of a quality education.

Besides, it is of the concerted opinion that existing models of teachings and curriculum in India are having several flaws that need corrective measures. These are as below if not limited to even:

(i) In technical education in India, today, teaching is imparted mostly to train 'how is 2+2= 4' rather than teaching, also, 'why is (2+2) not equal to 5'. In India, technical education is badly missing to have fair mix of "why and how" based education.

(ii) Till date in all Institutes/Universities it is found that teaching is mostly imparted only on documented knowledge available in books and in literature. Delivery of documented knowledge has taken away the whole space of "knowledge by realisation and knowledge of imagination". Curriculum development badly needs to address the missing link of igniting the thought process of the students.

(iii) Existing curriculum in all Institutes/Universities are decisively found to be creating engineers who will be job seekers only. Curriculum development requires to provide ample scope and space of making future generation job providers with fair amount of exposure, promotion and training in entrepreneurship practices, scopes and opportunities.

(iv) Existing curriculum is found to be lacking in producing technical engineers. More attention is often given on producing academic engineers. Subject papers like design contest, hardware design are missing in curriculum.

(v) It is further felt that for making complete human beings, students needs to have training on "mental soundness and physical fitness". Therefore the compulsory subjects like NCC, NSS, Yoga etc are made to be part of syllabi of every technical course.

(vi) Technical education in India is imparted in convention mode of teaching. It is proposed that subject papers of all courses should be divided into two to three groups;

(a) Theory based teaching (may be called S.N Base model of teaching) in which philosophy is "theory is the first practice"

(b) Practice based teaching (may be called J.C Bose model of teaching) in which philosophy is **"practice is the first theory".**

(c) I-Course which will be taught by industrial persons only.

(vii) Curriculum should be **linked to the examination process**. We must emphasize on changing examination that requires a system of evaluation for which we can know **"how much a student knows rather than how much he/she doesn't know"**. For constructive examination system, it will mix of **conventional examination, open book examination and online examination.**

(viii) All curriculum and syllabi must have defined **learning objectives and learning outcomes.**

Recently paradigm shifts in govt policies and priorities are noticed. MI, SI, DI, CI – Making India, Skilled India, Digital India, Clean India – promotion is undoubtedly a move to reckon with. In this move, the introduction of CBCS may be preferred to if choice of subject papers, credit system etc, are made appropriately and judiciously in curriculum development. At the same time, as autonomy is one of the pillars of quality, and as autonomy offers competitive advantages among competiting autonomies; it is essential that CBCS should be associated with adequate autonomy (Liberty & not Licence) to the Departments and Institutes/ Universities where expertise of the Members of Faculty of the Department or Universities/Institutes concerned will be the best guide for selection of the credits, number of choices of subject papers to be left to students in groups etc. It is also necessarily felt that the uniform audit or credit limit etc, for all concerned may not be a good idea as "Course is not for credit but credit is for courses" – which decisively needs the expertise of the Members of Faculty to decide upon.

Based on the above observations, a guideline and structure for B.Tech UG programme – (4 years) of Computer Science & Engineering under CBCS is given below (A) subject to further quality improvement by individual Department/Universities/ Institutes alongwith a sample subject content of a subject paper (B).

A. Sample Structure for 4-years B.Tech in CSE

Classification/ Grouping	Subject Papers	Credit Assignment	Choice of no. of Subject papers	Model of Teaching (J.C. Bose or S.N. Bose or I-Course teaching by Industrial Expert)	Type of courses	Remarks
Preparatory & Competency (inter-departmental)	1. Engineering Mathematics-I 2. Engineering Chemistry 3. Engineering Physics-I 4. Life Science 5. Engineering Mechanics 6. Engineering Drawing-I 7. Workshop Practice-I 8. Basic Electrical & Electronics Engineering 9. Philosophy in Engineering 10. Sociology in Engineering 11. History & Technology 12. Engineering Mathematics-II 13. Basic elements of Mechanical Engineering 14. Engineering Drawing II 15. Workshop Practice-II 16. Programming in C 17. Engineering Physics-II 18. Digital Electronics & Logic Design 19. Discrete Mathematics 20. Circuit Theory 21. Optimization Methods 22. Computational Numerical Methods 23. Principles of Communication Engineering 24. Control Engineering	Should be left to the Deptt. for ensuring ACADEMIC AUTONOMY of Deptt./Institute	Should be left to the Deptt. for ensuring ACADEMIC AUTONOMY of Deptt./Institute	Should be left to the Deptt. for ensuring ACADEMIC AUTONOMY of Deptt./Institute	CreditCredit	Preparatory Context

Discipline Competency (Compulsory + Elective)	1. Computer Organization & Architecture 2. Data Structure & Algorithm 3. Object Oriented Programming 4. Formal Languages & Automata 5. Advanced Computer Architecture 6. Microprocessors, Micro-controllers & Embedded System 7. Operating Systems 8. Design & Analysis of Algorithm. 9. Database Management systems 10. System Software & Administration 11. Graph Theory & Combinatories 12. Computer Networking 13. Software Networking 14. Computer Graphics & Multimedia Technology 15. Compiler Design 16. Internet & Web Technology 17. Web Design & Management 18. Programming C + + 19. Java Programming 20. Accounting Packages 21. Enterprise Resource Planning 22. Bio Informatics 23. Quantum Computing 24. Robotics 25. Data Mining & Warehousing 26. Data Compression 27. Real-time Systems 28. Software Project Management 29. Software Quality Engineering 30. Neural Networks 31. Fuzzy Systems 32. Parallel Algorithms 33. Real Time Operating Systems 34. Information Coding Techniques 35. Pattern Recognition & Image Processing 36. Embedded System Design 37. Digital Audio & System Process 38. Parallel Algorithms-II 39. Green Computing 40. Cloud Computing 41. Computational Complexity 42. Natural Language Processing 43. Information Security 44. AI & Neural Network	Should be left to the Deptt. for ensuring ACADEMIC AUTONOMY of Deptt./Institute	Should be left to the Deptt. for ensuring ACADEMIC AUTONOMY of Deptt./Institute	Should be left to the Deptt. for ensuring ACADEMIC AUTONOMY of Deptt./Institute	Credit	World Context

Communi-cation Skill Competency	1. Communication Skill 2. Any Regional Language (Indian) 3. Sanskrit 4. Foreign Language (French/Korean) 5. Foreign Language (German/Chinese) 6. Mass Communication for Technology	Should be left to the Deptt. for ensuring ACADEMIC AUTONOMY of Deptt./Institute	Should be left to the Deptt. for ensuring ACADEMIC AUTONOMY of Deptt./Institute	Should be left to the Deptt. for ensuring ACADEMIC AUTONOMY of Deptt./Institute	Credit	World Context
Behavioural Science & Environ-mental Awareness Competency	1. Environmental Science & Engineering 2. History of Science & Technology 3. Stochastic Process 4. Disaster Management 5. Green Technology 6. Behavioural Science	Should be left to the Deptt. for ensuring ACADEMIC AUTONOMY of Deptt./ Institute	Should be left to the Deptt. for ensuring ACADEMIC AUTONOMY of Deptt./ Institut	Should be left to the Deptt. for ensuring ACADEMIC AUTONOMY of Deptt./ Institute	Credit	World Context
MUST Competency	1. Application of Discipline Competency in Rural Technology 2. Society & Technology 3. Entrepreneurship & Innovation	Should be left to the Deptt. for ensuring ACADEMIC AUTONOMY of Deptt./ Institute	Should be left to the Deptt. for ensuring ACADEMIC AUTONOMY of Deptt./ Institute	Should be left to the Deptt. for ensuring ACADEMIC AUTONOMY of Deptt./ Institute		Indian Context
Physical, Mental & Ethical Competency	1. NCC/NSS 2. Values & Ethics 3. Yoga Practices 4. Games & Sports	Should be left to the Deptt. for ensuring ACADEMIC AUTONOMY of Deptt./ InstituteInstitute	Should be left to the Deptt. for ensuring ACADEMIC AUTONOMY of Deptt./ Institute	Should be left to the Deptt. for ensuring ACADEMIC AUTONOMY of Deptt./ Institute	Credit	Societal Context
Innovation, Design & Imagination Building Competency	1. Engineering Ethics & IPR 2. Creative Design 3. Research Paper Communication 4. Project Works 5. Seminar	Should be left to the Deptt. for ensuring ACADEMIC AUTONOMY of Deptt./ Institute	Should be left to the Deptt. for ensuring ACADEMIC AUTONOMY of Deptt./ Institute	Should be left to the Deptt. for ensuring ACADEMIC AUTONOMY of Deptt./ Institute	Credit	Indian Context
Industrial Adherence Competency	1. Industrial Management 2. Industrial Training. 3. Industrial Psychology 4. Nature & Industry 5. Marketing Management 6. IT Management	Should be left to the Deptt. for ensuring ACADEMIC AUTONOMY of Deptt./ Institute	Should be left to the Deptt. for ensuring ACADEMIC AUTONOMY of Deptt./ Institute	Should be left to the Deptt. for ensuring ACADEMIC AUTONOMY of Deptt./ Institute	Credit	Industri-al Context

Other (Optional) Competency Courses	1. Photography 2. Drawings 3. Article Writing	Should be left to the Deptt. for ensuring ACADEMIC AUTONOMY of Deptt./Institute	Should be left to the Deptt. for ensuring ACADEMIC AUTONOMY of Deptt./Institute	Should be left to the Deptt. for ensuring ACADEMIC AUTONOMY of Deptt./Institute	Audit (Pass or Fail)	Individual Professional Context

B. Sample Module/Course Content of a Subject Paper

Name of the Module: Programming in C

Module Code: CSE 201

Semester: 2nd

Credit Value: 4 [P=8, T=0, L=0]

Module Leader:

A. Objectives:

The course is designed to meet the objectives of:

1. introducing art, science and engineering of C programming language to the students of all UG programs,
2. teaching and training of different problems in data structures,
3. guiding and training students to write efficient coding,
4. guiding & training students to fragment problems into different functions or units.

B. Learning outcomes:

Students successfully completing this module will be able to:

1. understand the basic terminology used in computer programming
2. write, compile and debug programs in C language in different operating systems.
3. design programs involving decision structures, loops and functions.
4. use and apply the dynamics of memory by the use of pointers in engineering applications.

5. use and apply the differences between structure oriented and function oriented programming in programming applications.

C. Subject matter:

Unit I:

Basic Idea: Algorithm, Flowchart, Program, Top down approach, Procedure oriented etc.. Keyword & Identifiers: History & Importance of C, Basic structure of C programs, C fundamentals: The C character set identifier, Constants and keywords, data types & size, variable names, declaration, statement , C token, symbolic constent.

Operators and Expression: Arithmetic Operators, Relational Operators, Logical Operators, Assignment Operators, Increment & Decrement operators, Condition Operators, Bitwise Operators, Special operators, precedence of arithmetic operators.

Managing Input & output operations: using of printf( ) & scanf ( ).

Unit II:

Decision making: Simple If statement, if-else statement, nested if else statement, Switch statement, nested switch, the operator, goto statement.

Decision making & branching: while statement, do-while statement, for statement. Array

Unit III:

Array: Declaration, Initialization and processing One-dimension array, Two-dimension array and multi dimension array and their operations.

String & pointer: String: Operation on String without using library function and using library function. Pointer: Declaration of pointer variables, accessing the variable by using pointer, pointer increment and decrement operator, pointer and array.

Functions: Basic functions, function type, function with no argument & no return value, function with no argument but return value, function with argument & return value, Storage class identifier, Call by reference, Recursive function. Pointer to function.

Unit IV:

Structure & Union: Defining a structure, accessing of structure variable, structure and array, array within structure. Nested structure, structure & functions, Pointer & structure, Unions, Enum.

File management system: Advantage of using file, Open, close, read. write in the files, Operation on files.

Dynamic memory Allocation: use of Malloc, calloc, realloc, free. Library functions, Implementation of Linked list and their various operations.

The pre-processor: macro statements.

D. List of practicals: (Minimum eight experiments should be conducted by students)

1. Write a program to find the two's complement of a given binary sequence.
2. Write a program to find the addition of two integer numbers by using 2's complement arithmetic.
3. Write a program to perform subtraction using 2's complement method.
4. Write a program to find the n-bits even/odd parity hamming code for the given binary sequences of r-bits.
5. Write a program to design the full adder logic and display the sum and carry of the provided binary inputs.

6. Write a program to design the truth table for any given function.
7. Write a program to find the shortest paths between each nodes of the given graph.
8. Write a program to design the traffic rules of a Junction Railway station consist with finite number of platforms.
9. Write a program to find the optimal weighted spanning tree from a graph.
10. Write a program to create a circular linked list and traverse the all the nodes.
11. Calculate the value of power factor, using two wattmeter methods, the first reading of wattmeter is X W and that of second wattmeter is Z W, when the both the reading is positive.
12. From the experimental data of OCC (Open Circuit Characteristics) and SCC (Short Circuit Characteristics) of a 1-Φ transformer, write a program for determining the parameters for the equivalent circuit.
13. Write a program to implement the Bernoulli's Equation.
14. Write a program to determination of Cantilever Beam – Concentrated load P at any point.
15. Write a program to determine the shear strength of soil by Triaxial and direct shear method.
16. Write a mini project to store all records of students and search by their name, roll number or registration number.
17. Write a program to create, edit, open, delete a file and perform different operations accordingly.
18. Write a program to backup one file to another file.
19. Write a program to merge two files.
20. Write a mini project to control mouse cursor and display whether left, right or scroll happens.

E. Teaching/ Learning/ Practice pattern:

Teaching: 40%

Learning: 10%

Practice: 50%

F. Examination pattern:

1. Theoretical Examination: Open book and on line.
2. Practical Examination: Conduct Programming test and viva voice.

G. Reading lists:

Books

1. Kerninghan and Ritchie,—*The 'C'programming language* ||, Prentice Hall.
2. Yashavant P. Kanetkar,—*Let Us C* ||, Infinity Science Press, 2008.
3. Herbert Schildt,—C: *The Complete Reference* ||, McGraw-Hill Education, 2000.
4. Balaguruswamy,—*Programming In Ansi C,* 5E ||, Tata McGraw-Hill Education, 2011.
5. Govil, Agrawal, Mathur & Pathak,—*Computer Fundamentals and Programming in C*□, Jaipur Publication House (JPH)
6. M.T. Somashekara,—*Programming in C* ||, PHI Learning Pvt. Ltd., 2005.
7. Sinha&Sinha,—*Foundations of Computing* ||, BPB Publications, 2002.
8. J. B. Dixit,—*Computer Fundamentals and Programming in C*□, Firewall Media, 2009.
9. Stephen G. Kochan,—*Programming in C* ||, Addison-Wesley Professional, 2014.

10. K. N. King,—*C Programming: A Modern Approach* ||, W.W. Norton, 2010.
11. Zed Shaw,—*Learn C The Hard Way* ||, Addison Wesley Professional, 2015.
12. Steve Oualline,—*Practical C Programming*, 3rd Edition ||, O'Reilly Media, Inc., 2003.
13. Ajay Mittal,—*Programming In C: A Practical Approach* ||, Pearson Education India, 2010.
14. A.P.Godse, D.A.Godse,—*Computer Concepts and Programming in C* ||, Technical Publications, 2008.

Magazines:

1. *C/C++ Users,* CMP Media LLC Publication, United States.
2. EPS Software Corp/*CODE Magazine,* 6605 Cypresswood Drive, Suite 300 Spring, TX 77379.

Journals:

1. *Science of Computer Programming:* Methods of Software Design: Techniques and Applications, Elsevier, ISSN: 0167-6423
2. *Programming and Computer Software,* Springer, ISSN: 0361-7688.
3. *Dr. Dobb's Journal,* United Business Media Publication, United State,ISSN: 1044-789X
4. *Journal of C Language,* CMP Media LLC Publication, United States
5. C vu Journal, ACCU, UK.

CBCS shall not be accepted as a permanent replacement of the existing credit system. Rather it will be a good idea to put the CBCS on trial and subject to achieving quality expected out of the trial say after 4 years, replacement may be appropriately thought of. It is a matter of great worry that CBCS should not be 100% choice based as then it will be catasphoric for requirement of huge number of Members of Faculty. Rather in the trial stage, CBCS may be applied subject to meeting the choice offered; based on availability of teachers to cope-up with the options/choices put forward by students.

13

Required Paradigm shift from just quality to quality plus Innovation (Q to QI)

In the scenario of the policies and priorities of the government in "Make in India, Skilled India, Digital India and Clean India" (MISIDICI), the role of Technical Higher Education undoubtedly will be a factor to reckon with. The Higher Technical Education in the country accordingly needs a paradigm shift from quality assurance & control to an exercise of promoting quality and innovation synergetically. In the context, some of the pertaining issues are: reframing and redesigning syllabi, reshaping & re-orienting examination system, injecting innovation in teaching (Teaching with Research and Research with Teaching) and judicious & co-operative assessment of publications and quality control policies.

The importance given to the research publication published in "undoubtedly quality journals" of foreign countries and professional bodies of the foreign countries requires examination in the light of "Make in India" exercise. Mute question is why not to encourage and promote Indian journals like Indian journal of pure & applied physics, Indian journal of pure physics, Journals of Electronics & Telecommunication Engineers and Journals of Institution of Engineers India! Why most important research carried out by distinguished Professors in India should not be published in Indian journals for promotion/ innovation and promotion to publish Indian path breaking research in Indian journals and thereby to make the journals at par (or even above) with other established journals of foreign countries is one of essential exercise for "Make in India"! A planned and concerted effort from all concerned (Government, Institutes, Universities Editors of journals) is now essential to bringing up research publication in Indian journals. One suggested innovation will be each Indian selected pool of journal should identify one published paper in each issue as Best Paper. Any faculty publishing minimum of 50 such best papers will be made Director/Vice-Chancellor on research-rewarded reserved post. Such reservation say 20% of Director/Vice-Chancellors positions may be called quality reservation rather than "in-equality" creating reservation.

As conventional means of quality assurance of publication acceptance and rejection of the papers needs innovation. Implementation of some novel innovations is required to enhance the quality of reviewing itself. Many reviewers are found to be inconsistent and inaccurate. An experience shows that in a review process a reviewer mixed up AVK with AKE and rejected a very good paper later accepted in another superior journal. Similarly, a reviewer mixed up error control between node to node with error control in end to end and rejected a Paper. With due respect to the reviewers and with due respect to the reviewing process, it will not be unjust if the reviewing process is made transparent and academic constructive debate based, whereupon on 1st reviewing, authors will have the right to challenge, if any of the comments of reviewer. Based on this academic debate and challenges next reviewing may be done with 2nd set of reviewers. Based on review results of the 2nd reviewing process and the academic debate in the 1st reviewing process Editorial Board may come to a decision that be reasonably superior decision. This will provide a better innovative platform for quality assurance.

It is proposed, the Editorial Board of Indian Journals of repute may think of the innovation and may apply the same to show the world that we are in the process of "Make in India" and not just follow the world.

For ensuring and enhancing quality of teaching in Technical Higher Education, it has become of paramount importance to think of different approaches rather than the conventional practices of students feedback and self appraisal assessment. Students feedback considerably acts in favour of cheap popularity of teachers rather than solid and sound teachers. Self appraisal in most cases is found to be superficial or exaggerated. As an innovative measure, the quality teaching may be improved and properly assessed by methods of examining "Academic Exercise" undertaken by teachers before teaching for which, possibly a format as given below may have to be mandatorily filled in by the teachers before teaching in each academic session for each of the subjects the teacher is supposed to teach:

Exercises Proposed for teaching in (July – December, 2015 Semester)

1. Name of the Teacher ____________________
2. Department ____________________
3. Course Title ____________________
4. Course code ____________________
5. Course Hands out (in reference to framed & approved syllabus) (maximum 500 words) ____________________

   ____

   ____

6. Books/Literature to be followed:

   (a) Books (Min. 2 texts + 3 references)

   (i) Title ____________

   Author ____________

Publisher ______________

Edition ______________

(ii) Title ______________

Author ______________

Publisher ______________

Edition ______________

(iii) Title ______________

Author ______________

Publisher ______________

Edition ______________

(iv) Title ______________

Author ______________

Publisher ______________

Edition ______________

(v) Title ______________

Author ______________

Publisher ______________

Edition ______________

(b) Magazines/Journals (Minimum 5)

(i)

(ii)

(iii)

(iv)

(v)

7. Mode of Teaching: J.C Bose/S. N. Bose (please tick).

8. If the course is of practices, list the experiments to be offered.

(i)
(ii)
(iii)
(iv)
(v)
(vi)
(vii)
(viii)

Are the manuals ready for the experiments to be conducted?

Yes/No (please tick)

If "No", the reasons thereof and fixing responsibility

____

____

____

____

Remarks/ Endorsement by the HoD With his /her signature with date	Name of the Teacher: Designation: Signature with Date:

This may be called pre-teaching assessment and quality assurance. For post-teaching assessment, decisively, the quality of question papers set by the teachers (in terms of type of the question set, the portion of the syllabus covered by questions, novelty in setting questions etc.) may be carefully examined and necessary feedback may be given to the teachers.

For promotion and generation of skilled India, there is felt that some sort of innovative practices to be exercised in Higher Technical Education. Several proposals may be thought of:

Teaching in selected subjects in each semester may be made in an environment of "Learn while doing" meaning that do practice and learn in the way from the first day.

The system of students internship once or twice in a 4-years Bachelor degree programme of engineering requires a re-look. Rather than internship, the period may be extended for the students for a semester to do an industrial project on industrial fellowship for which industries may be requested to provide avenues & opportunities to the students.

For industrial flavor and for industrial oriented teaching, it may be a good exercise that summer vacation of two months for teachers may be curtailed to one month and remaining one month may be made compulsory for teachers to go to industries for being acquinted with industrial flavour and industrial requirement for skilled human resources. Some sort of resistance will always be there for promulgating this new scheme for making a new India, but discussions and deliberations may be initiated. The proposal is to benefit teachers and students fraternity. It is to a large extent sure that if the teachers get training in industry during vacation, it will be beneficial for getting industrial supported research projects and consultancy work. Not only that, such industrial training may improve their professional career.

14

Salient points of QS University Rankings: BRICS 2015

Recently QS University Rankings: BRICKS (Brazil, Russia, India, China & South Africa) project has published the ranking of Universities in the countries of BRICS. Eight indicators namely academic reputation (30%), employer reputation (20%), Faculty/Student ratio (20%), staff with Ph.D (10%), paper per faculty (10%), citation per paper (5%), International faculty (2.5) and International Students (2.5%) were the parameters to decide the ranking. The ranking published shows that India has a very good place in Higher Education in the BRICS. A table of Indian Universities within 200 rank is shown below:

Top University / Institute of India as per QS University Rankings: BRICS 2015

Institute / University	Rank	Central / State / Private	State where University/Institute is located
Indian Institute of Science (IISc) Bangalore	5	Central	Karnataka
Indian Institute of Technology, Delhi	13	Central	Delhi
Indian Institute of Technology, Bombay	16	Central	Maharashtra
Indian Institute of Technology, Kanpur	18	Central	Uttar Pradesh
Indian Institute of Technology, Madras	20	Central	Tamil Nadu
Indian Institute of Technology, Kharagpur	24	Central	West Bengal
University of Delhi	46	Central	Delhi
Indian Institute of Technology, Guwahati	50	Central	Assam
University of Calcutta	52	State	West Bengal

(Contd..)

(Contd..)

University of Mumbai	58	State	Maharashtra
University of Madras	78	State	Tamil Nadu
Banaras Hindu University	93	Central	Uttar Pradesh
Birla Institute of Technology and Science, Pilani	95	Private	Rajasthan
Manipal University (Manipal Academy of Higher Education)	97	Private	Karnataka
University of Calicut	109	State	Kerala
University of Pune	110	State	Maharashtra
Aligarh Muslim University, Aligarh	111	Central	Uttar Pradesh
National Institute of Technology, Rourkela	113	Central	Odisha
University of Kashmir, Srinagar	140	State	Jammu & Kashmir
Amity University	142	Private	Punjab
G.B. Pant University of Agriculture and Technology, Pantnagar	144	Central	Uttarakhand
University of Mysore	149	State	Karnataka
Amrita Vishwa Vidyapeetham	151	Private	Tamil Nadu
Andhra University	152	State	Andhra Pradesh
Anna University	153	State	Tamil Nadu
Bharathidasan University	156	State	Tamil Nadu
Dr. Harisingh Gour University (University of Sagar), Sagar	161	Central	Madhya Pradesh
Jadavpur University	165	State	West Bengal
Punjab University	174	State	Punjab
VIT University	198	Private	Tamil Nadu

Based on the table, following pertaining issues may be thought of:

- Thirteen Central Universities and twelve State Universities are placed within the 200 rank. It is correctly known that State funding is measurably less compared to Central funding for the Universities. Even then performance of the State Universities is found to be commendable as per the current ranking. This decisively calls for funding to the State Universities particularly the Universities ranked within the 200 position liberally by the Central Govt. Such Central assistance may be in the form of ad-hoc development grant per year to make these State Universities to be at par with the Central Universities in the rank. This approach may make India really global in Higher Education in equitable manner.
- Among the State Universities, the University of Calcutta is at the top in the ranking and among the private

universities, Birla Institute of Science & Technology, Pilani is at the top. Both these universities are oldest in respective sector of "State" and "Private", and as if "Old is Gold".

- Universities in the states of Karnataka, Delhi, Maharashtra, Uttar Pradesh, Tamil Nadu, West Bengal, Rajasthan, Kerela, Odisha, Punjab, Jammu & Kashmir and Madhya Pradesh are found in the rank of 200 in this ranking. Universities located in the other states therefore need special support guidance and direction from the State and Central Govt. to make them at par with other universities so as to reduce the geographical developmental gap in Higher Education.
- The presence of five private universities within the 200 rank conclusively establishes that in future ,role of private universities in India in imparting quality Higher Education cannot be ignored.
- The Ministry of Human Resource Development, Govt. of India, of late, elevated the then Regional Engineering Colleges to National Institutes of Technology as well established a few new National Institutes of Technology with objective of making them at par with International Universities. The presence of National Institute of Technology, Rourkela within 200 rank is felt to be meeting the desired National objective.
- The ranking of QS University Ranking BRICS 2015 greatly differs from those published in various Indian Magazines. This is a matter of dispute to be resolved.
- Disturbances and instability are the stumbling blocks for development. Yet then position of University of Kashmir within 200 rank definitely suggests that the development process may not be so curbed if devotion and determination are delegated. This university in real term has converted "Difficulties into opportunities".

- There is seen some wide mismatch between NAAC/NBA accredited status and the current BRICS ranking of Indian Universities. There is a need therefore to locate and identify the issues of mismatch and to initiate measure to correct the process either of the ways.

Index